Six Lessons for Success

Six Lessons for Success

Bob Willoughby

ISBN: 978-0-578-23544-8

For Bobby and Kristen, and to my grandchildren yet unborn.
—Father's Day, June 21, 2015

Introduction

If you can't explain it simply, you don't
understand it well enough.
—Albert Einstein

Success is not a recent phenomenon. In fact, success and the concept of being successful is as old as human history itself. We know this because the topic of being good at things can be traced back to the origin of the written word and beyond that in the proverbs and teachings of the ancients. The principles of successful living are not exclusive to any one particular group, gender, or type of individual. They are present across every culture and form of humanity. Interestingly while the world has changed dramatically and people have evolved over time, the behaviors and attitudes of successful individuals have remained relatively constant for centuries. Why is that? Why are some of the most successful people in recent years still talking about the same things that successful people who lived over two thousand years ago talked about?

The answer for me is straightforward. While technological advances make life very different today, the core principles of successful living have not changed. That opinion on its face value may not seem controversial, but I'm certain that there would be no shortage of new age thinkers who would disagree. However, the most honest of them must concede that the so-called new concepts they are endorsing have their basis in these eternal truths. I do concur that there is always room for innovation and improvement, but I believe that these fundamentals will be found within those advancements, whatever they might happen to be. For the record, I lay no personal claim of discovery of these ideas. This information has been around much longer than I have and has been explored by some of the greatest minds in history. My role is to collect and examine the similarities of their thoughts and leave them to you to evaluate their validity.

In writing this book, I committed to a few goals. The first of these is centered in the Hippocratic philosophy of do no harm. I'm confident that the advice given in *Six Lessons for Success* can only benefit anyone who chooses to accept it. The second goal follows the credo of the outdoors: Leave your campsite better than you found it. In this case the campsite is you, the reader. There is so much negative information being circulated in the world these days that it is important to me personally to put forth only positive ideas and content. I humbly submit that if you choose to read this book and consider the concepts and quotes contained within these pages, you will be better off for having done so.

Six Lessons for Success is dedicated to my children and (hopefully) their children one day. I strongly believe in these fundamentals, and I know that they will work for them no matter what they attempt to do in their lives. I'm equally positive that they will work for you should you choose to study and use them.

While do no harm and leave people better than you found them are the primary goals, I had a few others that I wanted to accomplish: Deliberately, I did not want the book to be overly long. The reason for this is because it's my belief that successful people generally don't overcomplicate things. I believe that they do powerful yet simple things repeatedly and with great focus. That being the case, it felt slightly inauthentic to me to write a lengthy book about the process of success. In addition, I wanted *Six Lessons for Success* to take the form of a story or a fable, not a dry textbook to struggle through or leave on a shelf. Some of my favorite books, such as *One Minute Manager, Rich Dad Poor Dad, The Little Red Book, Chicken Soup for the Soul, The Energy Bus*, and *Who Moved My Cheese*, involve powerful concepts woven into stories. I don't think there is any coincidence that they are so widely read. Also, historically, people have used stories to teach lessons, so this seemed like an obvious choice for me to make.

The parable in *Six Lessons for Success* focuses on a father and son, although it could represent any sort of teaching relationship, such as a manager and employee, coach and player, or teacher and student. It is not an autobiographical account, but there are elements of different relationships that I have had in my life. I suppose that while I represent neither the father nor the son, the most accurate description would be to say that parts of me are in both of them. I would not be surprised if you recognized parts of yourself in each of the characters as well.

The father and son were close as the child was growing up but grew apart in the young man's teen and college years. They begin to realize as the son is becoming an adult that they miss each other and need each other. There is vital information that they need to share about life and becoming successful in the real world that they have not yet discussed. The story finds them at the beginning of their journey toward having this conversation and repairing that relationship.

So exactly who is *Six Lessons for Success* written for and how should they use it? This book is written for both teachers and students of the success process. It is meant to be used as a reference for readers to use as an ongoing resource. Each chapter is constructed as a different lesson. After discussing each specific lesson, the father and the son share inspirational quotes that apply. The son then recaps the key learning points of each lesson in his own notebook. There is space at the end of each chapter for the reader to include their own quotes and key points that have personal meaning to them. There are also brief exercises that are related to each lesson to complete. The rationale for that is that it is important for readers to become students themselves of the *Six Lessons for Success* in order to apply them to their own success journey. So you will literally be cowriting your own version of the book with me, and your book won't be finished until we hear from you on the subject!

Six Lessons for Success is not meant to be kept pristinely unmarked and in perfect condition. Instead, it is meant to be creased and dog-eared with notes and personal observations written throughout its pages. By the time each reader is done, they will have created their own individualized success handbook that they can return to whenever needed.

Significantly, you will not find reference in *Six Lessons for Success* as to what *success is*. We allow the reader to determine that for themselves. Indeed, the concept of what success means is relative to each individual and situation. So in a very real sense, *Six Lessons for Success* is not a philosophy book; it's an instruction manual for people who are trying to learn what they need to do to achieve their goals and gain insight into how successful people think and behave. Once you have this information, it will be easier for you to distinguish successful traits in yourself and others and apply them to your own circumstances.

I hope you enjoy reading *Six Lessons for Success*, and I wish you success as you start your journey.

Be well,

Bob Willoughby

The Father

The father looked at his watch. He was nervous. The son would be arriving to meet him in five minutes. *This is crazy*, he thought, *Why am I so anxious about seeing my own child?* Deep down he understood why. To say that their relationship had become strained in the past few years would be an understatement. Things had not always been that way; this was a more recent development.

When the boy was young, they were very close, nearly inseparable. The son had been a promising athlete, and the two would spend hours together playing and practicing the sports they loved. They also had long talks about the meaning of life. Both were deep thinkers who enjoyed that sort of thing. The father was not the type of person who believed that adults should talk down to children. He spoke to the son as an adult and asked him what his opinions were and why he felt that way. Almost always he was impressed with the young man's intuitive grasp of people, situations, and occurrences. The son seemed wise beyond his years, and he did what he could as a parent to nurture that and develop the son's confidence.

In his early teens, the young man got to travel and see how other people lived. He learned how fortunate he was and that it was important to give back and help others. The father was deeply moved by the son's compassion for people. He just knew that the son was destined to do great things with his life. As the years went by, however, the communication that had always been so effortless between them became increasingly difficult. The young man with the bright future began to make some dangerous choices and some very poor decisions. Unfortunately, the father did not handle the situation well at all. He became angry, confused, and hurt by the son's attitude and behavior. At times the father was at a loss for words, and he completely shut down. Other times he tried to help the boy understand the mistakes he was making with his life, and things would escalate into huge emotional arguments that left him drained. The father tried everything he could think of and secretly hoped that, somehow, the son would come to his senses and get himself back on track, but he felt that the older the boy got, the less likely it seemed that it would happen. The father was very worried about the young man's future. Eventually there was a final, ugly fight between the two. The details of the disagreement or who was right and who was wrong were not that important. They had basically been having the same quarrel for years anyway. The father felt that there was nothing he could say to his angry son that he would understand. The son felt that the father would not listen and didn't love and encourage him anymore. Except for the occasional text message, they did not communicate for quite some time.

During that span, the father felt just as lost as the son. Outwardly he was a successful businessman who ran a large company. He was known for being the type of individual who developed people and guided them toward success. Friends, family members, and employees came to him often to ask for advice. While he was always happy to help them, he secretly felt like a failure because he could not help the person in his life whom he desperately wanted to help and who needed his guidance most. He felt that he had become a person who outwardly found success, but inwardly he felt like an impostor. Then something interesting happened. After a year of minimal contact, the son reached out to him. He wanted to meet face-to-face.

The Son

The son looked at the time on his phone. Ten minutes ago, the alert had notified him that he had fifteen minutes before seeing the father. Not that he needed any reminding. He was usually very tense anytime they got together, and this time was no exception. He had not always felt that way, however. When he was a kid, the father was literally his best friend. He looked forward to spending time with his dad every day. He could always count on him to give it to him straight, although, if truth be told, he did not always understand or care for the father's brand of "tough love."

As a kid he had excelled easily at most things he tried. However, after he entered high school, things became more difficult. He became less interested in achieving his potential and more interested in fitting in with the high school crowd.

In an effort to gain acceptance with his new friends, he made some poor choices. It did not help matters that the father was not pleased by this. The boy who was used to achieving was not transitioning well to adulthood; in fact, he was struggling. He felt like the father did not understand his troubles and wasn't there for him anymore. The more he struggled, the angrier he became and the more reckless and self-destructive. While he was able to finish high school and get accepted at a small college, he knew that he was not living up to his potential. In fact, he did not even want to go to college. He did it for two reasons: it allowed him to get away from his dad, and he didn't know what else to do. He was going through the motions, and he knew it. Things continued this way until, one day, he and the father had a big fight. He felt like he had no direction, but he was tired of being pushed toward a future that he had not quite figured out yet. So he pushed back—hard.

For a long time, they barely communicated with each other, but during that time a transformation began to occur. Completely on his own and apart from the father, the son began to make changes in his life. They were small changes at first, but they were steps in the right direction. With each positive step, his confidence, while still fragile, began to grow. He began to take his education seriously and even made the dean's list one semester. He became more active and got into great shape again. It was as if the seeds that had been planted in him long ago had begun to germinate and take root. He realized as he began to fulfill more of his potential that he was less angry with the father. In fact, as much as he hated to admit it, he wanted to tell him that he was doing well.

While he was proud of the progress he had made on his own, he still wanted to be acknowledged by the man who had been the central figure of his childhood. There was something else bothering him also. He was growing anxious about his pending graduation. Soon he would be facing a whole new set of challenges, and he wondered if he was ready. To him it seemed as if the working world was a mystery he had no idea how to solve. He thought of his dad and all their conversations over the years. He felt like he was doing better than before, but he still had a long way to go, so he decided to ask the father to meet him at a small coffee shop near his office. Before he could change his mind, he composed a short text message and hit *send*.

The Meeting

The father was pleasantly surprised by the son's invitation, and he confirmed he would be there with cautious optimism. By the day of the meeting, however, that optimism had turned into anxiety. He had not had any meaningful contact with the son in over a year, and the one time that they had met had ended with an angry confrontation. *How was this meeting going to turn out?* he wondered. It had the potential to be just as awkward and uncomfortable as the previous one.

When the son entered the coffee shop, he saw that the father had already arrived and was seated at a table with two steaming cups of coffee. The father smiled and extended his hand. "Good to see you, son," he said. "How are you?"

"Not bad," the son replied coolly. "I'm doing a lot better than I was the last time we talked."

It's true, the father thought. He could see that the young man had gotten himself together. He seemed sharp and focused, not at all like the confused, angry young man that had caused him such frustration over the last few years. But there was something else the father could sense as well: a detached formality that had not been there before. He quickly realized that this was not going to be an emotional reunion. Instead, it had the uneasy feel of a business meeting.

"I'm glad you wanted to get together, son," he said, pressing on. "I can tell you have something you would like to discuss. What's on your mind?"

"I won't sugarcoat it," the son began. "I don't think much of the way you have treated me the past few years. Quite frankly, you've been a real jerk."

The father was not surprised by the son's harsh words, but they stung all the same. Rather than react, however, he stayed calm. He knew that the young man had more to say. "I'm pretty clear about how you feel," he replied with a slight grin. "You said all that and more the last time I saw you. Somehow I don't think you contacted me after a year to tell me that again."

The father's placid reaction confused the son. He had just insulted the man, but instead of getting angry as he would have in the past, he was smiling. Something was going on, but he wasn't sure what it could be. "I've made a lot of changes in my life," the young man continued, "and, without any help from you, I have put myself in position to graduate from college."

"That's wonderful," the older man said, "I have no words to describe how proud I am of you."

"Wait a minute," the son said angrily. "You didn't help me one bit in the past year! We barely communicated! How dare you say you are proud of me! I did this for me, not to make you proud."

A bitter silence hung between the two of them for a minute that seemed to last for an eternity. Finally, the father said softly, "That is why I'm so proud of you. You did this for yourself and not for anyone else. This will be your accomplishment and not something anyone can ever take from you. However, your diploma in and of itself won't do anything for you. The most important thing about it is the effort and the dedication it took to earn it and what you learned about yourself along that journey." He took a long sip of coffee to allow his words to sink in, then he continued. "Unfortunately, many people spend their entire lives trying to gain the approval of others, which is a near certain way to guarantee their own unhappiness. It took me many years to learn that. I am impressed that you figured it out so young. You had some very good excuses not to finish your education, but I guess you decided that it was actually important to you that you complete it."

The son shifted uncomfortably in his chair. "I'll admit that you are right about that, Dad. The entire time you were pushing me to change, I just couldn't find the motivation to get it done. When we were not talking, I realized it was up to me to sink or swim."

The father looked at the son's face and thought he saw a glimmer of recognition in his eyes. It was almost as if he was having that realization as he spoke.

"I think we both learned a powerful lesson, son," he said thoughtfully. "I began to understand that I couldn't want something for you that you didn't want for yourself. I did the best I could to teach you when you were younger, but ultimately it was your decision to make these changes." The father thought back to that difficult time, one of the most challenging of his life. He knew that he needed to let go and give the son the opportunity to either succeed or fail on his own. All his attempts to push him in the direction he had wanted him to go had failed miserably.

"At first I was just angry with you because I felt you were giving up on me," the son said, "and I wanted to prove you wrong. But after a while, those feelings began to fade, and new ones began to emerge. I started to enjoy what I was doing and started feeling good about myself again."

The father nodded his head knowingly. He had seen this often with his employees. He believed it was a basic human trait that people feel stuck when they are focused on a problem or a conflict and that they only begin to feel good again when they start to take positive action to fix things. "I'm glad you are regaining your confidence," he said, smiling, "but somehow I don't think that is what you came to tell me either."

The young man sat back in his chair and sighed. It irritated him when the father was right. He took a deep breath and then he began. "The reason I wanted to speak with you is because I want your advice. For as long as I can remember, people have come to you for guidance. It seems to me that many of those people have become successful after working with you. Now that I'm about to become a graduate, I was wondering if you could teach me what you taught them."

It was now the father's turn to lean back in his chair. The son was actually asking for his help! While he had always dreamed of this conversation happening, he was caught slightly off guard now that it was. He took a moment to collect his thoughts before answering. He knew that how he responded would play a pivotal role in how things would unfold moving forward. "I would be honored to help you," he said. "I have always felt that you are a tremendously talented individual, but I will admit that there were many times that I had my doubts you would ever attempt to reach your potential. I'm glad you want to try, but there are a few things I should clarify before we begin."

The son studied the father intently. "What are your conditions?" he asked.

"Well, they aren't actually conditions as much as they are things that you will need to understand before I can help you," the father explained. "I can teach you what I know. I can inspire you with words, actions, and beliefs, but what I cannot do is motivate you."

"I'm confused," the son said. "You can teach and inspire me, but you can't motivate me? Aren't they the same thing?"

"I can see why you might think that," the father said. "They are very similar but not the same. Knowledge that is taught and words that inspire come from external sources. Motivation, on the other hand, is an internal resource. I can't motivate you because the only person who can motivate you is *you*."

The son had never thought about it in those terms before. "So what you are saying is that I can learn and be inspired by others, but I must supply my own motivation."

"Exactly," said the father, "and the level to which you are motivated will be the single biggest factor in determining how successful you ultimately become. Anyone who looks to someone else for motivation is bound to be disappointed."

"What about parents, teachers, and bosses?" the young man asked. "Isn't it their responsibility to motivate?"

"That is a common belief held by many people who are

not successful," replied the father. "But successful people don't think that way. They understand that their personal success is no one else's responsibility."

The two sat together in silence for a moment, sipping their coffee. The son was the first to break the silence. "That's interesting," he said. "So it's your opinion that successful people actually think differently than people who are not as successful?"

"That's exactly what I'm saying," the father agreed. "Let's consider it for a moment. As long as there have been people, some have been able to accomplish more than others. I'm even convinced that there were cavemen and women who thought differently and were extremely successful!"

They shared a laugh thinking about what a "successful" caveman might be like. They joked about how he would be able to make his own fire, have more to eat, and live in a safer, dryer place than the other cavemen in his neighborhood. It was the first time they'd laughed together in years. It felt slightly awkward, but also good. The son had to admit that while the father's analogy seemed ridiculous at face value, there was a certain validity to it. Logically, it must be true he reasoned, or we would still be living the same way as our ancestors. Someone at some point had to figure out a better way, which would mean they had a different viewpoint than the others.

"I know that sounds crazy," the father said, "and I certainly don't claim to have scientific proof on the subject. My point is that there have always been successful people; it's not a new phenomenon. I also believe that successful people throughout history share distinctly similar behaviors and that these behaviors will continue to make those who practice them successful for years to come."

This was the information the son had come for. "All right then," he said. "What is it that successful people do that is different?"

The father smiled with approval. "Outstanding question; to understand that we must shift our focus away from the accomplishments of successful individuals and begin to study what they think about and say on the subject." He paused to finish the last of his coffee, then continued. "Fortunately, as we have discussed, history is full of examples of successful people to support our research. There are also successful individuals from more recent times that we can study. We then need to evaluate the commonalities of their thoughts and apply them to your efforts."

"Excuse me for saying so, but that seems like it would be an incredibly broad topic," the son said. "How will we begin to figure all of that out?"

"By focusing on the six primary things all high achievers focus on. I call them the Six Lessons," the father replied.

The son was intrigued. "The Six Lessons?" he asked. "OK, then what are they?"

"If you are interested in learning them, meet me here next week at the same time for the First Lesson," the father said as he rose from the table. He then reached into his briefcase and pulled out an unused composition notebook. "I would like you to use this book to take notes and capture your key learning points each time we meet. I think you will find it to be a very valuable use of your time as we go through this process."

The son stoically accepted the father's gift. He was willing to do whatever was required to complete the Six Lessons. Then he stood, and the two men shook hands in a robotic manner, each secretly relieved that the meeting had not been a complete disaster.

After the father exited the coffee shop, the son returned to the table, opened his new composition notebook to the first page, and created the following list:

Key Learning Points

- People who try to accomplish goals for the approval of others usually wind up unhappy.
- You cannot convince someone to want something that they do not want. They must choose it for themselves.
- People only begin to feel good when they start taking action to solve their problems.
- You can be inspired by others, but motivation comes from within.
- Your level of motivation is the single biggest factor in determining your success.
- Throughout history, many successful people have believed similar things.

The First Lesson: Commit to Goals

*What you get by achieving your goals is not as important as
what you become by achieving your goals.*
—Henry David Thoreau

The week went by slowly for the son. Although he had a
tough time admitting it to himself, he had enjoyed recon-
necting with his dad. He was energized by the conversation and
intrigued by the idea of the Six Lessons. He reported to the
coffee shop at the appointed time the following week and found
that the father had already arrived. "Have a seat," the older man
said, motioning to the chair across from him. The son noticed a
small stack of index cards sitting on the table.

"What are the cards for?" he asked.

The father smiled. "They aren't just cards; they are today's
research." The father then pulled the top index card from the
stack and handed it to the son. "Please read this aloud."

The son studied the card for a moment and began:

*"It is not the critic who counts; not the man who points out
how the strong man stumbles, or where the doer of deeds could have
done them better. The credit belongs to the man who is actually in
the arena, whose face is marred by dust and sweat and blood; who*

strives valiantly; who errs, who comes short again and again, because there is no effort without error and shortcoming; but who does actually strive to do the deeds; who knows great enthusiasms, the great devotions; who spends himself in a worthy cause; who at the best knows in the end the triumph of high achievement, and who at the worst, if he fails, at least fails while daring greatly, so that his place shall never be with those cold and timid souls who neither know victory nor defeat."

When the son had finished, he looked up and thought he could see the trace of a tear in the older man's eyes. "That is an amazing quote," he said. "Did you write that or something? Is that why you are crying?"

The father chuckled softly then waved him off. "That is one of my favorite quotes," he said, "and to hear my child read such powerful words causes me to feel slightly emotional." He composed himself briefly and continued. "This quote actually came from a speech given by Theodore Roosevelt back in 1910. He was a powerful achiever who accomplished many things in his life, including becoming president, winning the Nobel Peace Prize, and protecting millions of acres of American wilderness as a conservationist. I'm curious, what do you think he meant by this statement?"

The son pondered the index card and said, "I think what he is saying is that, win or lose, it's important to try. I also think he is saying there will always be people who criticize your efforts, and you should not let them bother you."

"Absolutely," said the father, "but I think he is also saying one additional thing. Even though he never actually uses the words, Roosevelt is talking about the importance of committing to goals, and that is the First Lesson."

The young man shrugged his shoulders casually and did not look particularly impressed. "OK, so the First Lesson is to set goals. Isn't that a little basic?"

"I can see by your response that you are a bit under-whelmed," the father chuckled and said, "and I probably should have warned you before we started that the Six Lessons are in no way complex. However, I did not say to *set* goals; I said to *commit* to goals. There is a huge difference." The father paused for a moment for effect and to allow his words to sink in, then he continued. "You see, the moment you commit to a goal, you go from being a passive observer to being a passionate participant, and that one change is what allows things to start happening for you."

The son gave him a puzzled look and said, "I'm not sure I understand. Could you explain to me the difference between having goals and committing to them?"

"OK, let's examine it for a minute," the father said. "Un-derstand that for all of the talk of goals, the largest group of people out there have no goals at all or have been given goals by someone else that they don't care about. This is problematic because without a goal they are excited about, they lack focus, so it is nearly impossible for them to accomplish anything. They are not participating, so nothing *can* happen. The next group of people is a little smaller. These are the individuals who have set goals for themselves. It is very easy to spot them; they tend to say things like 'someday I might,' or 'I'd really like to,' or 'I wish I could.' These individuals may be slightly better off be-cause they have some focus, but the same lack of action basically makes them no more effective than the first group. The final and smallest group of people are those who commit themselves to a goal. They're also easy to spot. They say things like, 'I'm going to be president of the company by the time I'm fifty,' or 'I'm taking my spouse to Europe for our twenty-fifth anniversary,' or 'I'm going to make my high school team this year.' Sometimes they say nothing at all, but you can see their commitment in their focus, desire, and work ethic."

"I think I see what you mean," the son replied. "People who set goals almost sound like they are hoping something will happen for them. People that commit to goals sound a lot more specific and confident that it will happen within a certain time frame, but is that enough?"

"I can understand your skepticism," the father said. "It does seem as if there should be more to it, doesn't it? Here is where the important distinction is: When you fully commit yourself to a goal, it literally has the ability to change your behavior. It causes you to ask yourself, *OK, now what?* And the answer is: create a plan and take specific action toward reaching the goal. We call this living goal committed."

"So having a goal is easy, but committing to it is where the difficulty lies," the son said. "It requires you to define what you want, set a time frame, create a plan, and take specific action."

"Exactly," said the father. "For example, let's say that we were to give a child a ball and ask her to throw it. That's a simple enough task that most kids can accomplish with ease. But then let's suppose that the same child decides to throw the ball and try to hit a specific target. This changes everything about her focus and concentration."

"That is a good analogy," the son agreed. "Besides, what fun is it to just throw a ball and not try to control where it goes? It's much more fun to try and hit the target."

"Correct," said the father. "Goals are basically just targets anyway. Hitting them is both rewarding and fulfilling; however, it is not necessarily the most critical thing."

The son looked at his old man like he had two heads. "What could be more important than accomplishing your goals?" he asked incredulously. "Isn't that what we are talking about?"

The father became serious for a moment, paused, and then earnestly said, "No, we are talking about the importance of *committing*, because the most important thing is what happens to us as people when we commit and strive to reach our goals and what we become through those efforts. You see, a person who lives a goal-committed life operates differently from a person who does not. When an individual is committed to a goal, it automatically focuses their behavior on what they want to make happen. Conversely, a person who is not committed does not act and tends to be fearful of negative outcomes."

"It seems to me that what you are saying is living a goal-committed life causes us to grow, regardless of whether we accomplish the objective," the son mused. "We can't lose because we either win or learn and get better." He took a sip of coffee as the father nodded in agreement. "It really all starts right there," the son said. "I can't get where I want to be without first having a goal and then committing to it."

"I know that it seems painfully obvious, but the first step of being successful is figuring out what you want to accomplish and then going after it with everything you've got. Only then are you truly living," said the father. He then handed the son the remaining index cards. "Please read these quotes aloud now."

The son read:

The greater danger for most of us isn't that we aim too high and we miss it, but that we aim too low and achieve it.

—Michelangelo

I've never had a single moment of depression
because I know my cause will triumph.

—Nelson Mandela

An average person with average talents, ambition, and average education can outstrip the most brilliant genius in our society if that person has clear, focused goals.

—Mary Kay Ash

Goals are pure fantasy unless you have a
specific plan to achieve them.

—Stephen Covey

Give me a stock clerk with a goal, and I will give you a man who will make history. Give me a man with no goals, and I will give you a stock clerk.

—J. C. Penney

If you're not in the arena also getting your ass kicked, I'm not interested in your feedback.

—Brené Brown

As he read the final index card, the son said, "I can now see your point about success not being a new phenomenon. It seems that people have been talking about the importance of committing to goals for a very long time."

"Exactly," the father said in agreement, "and there are literally thousands of successful people throughout history who said very similar things. Amazing coincidence, right?"

The son smiled at the father's sarcasm, while silently admitting to himself that he had made his point quite effectively.

The father then said, "The lesson is not quite over, however. You will have homework to complete."

"Homework?" asked the son. "What would you like me to do?"

"Your task is to go out and find six quotes about committing to goals that have meaning to you. I'd like you to bring them back and share them with me. Can you meet me here tomorrow morning at the same time?"

The son said he would, and the two shook hands. He then hustled out of the coffee shop, eager to take on his new task and curious about where his pursuits in the upcoming twenty-four hours would lead him.

The next morning, he was back at the coffee shop well before the appointed time, and he'd brought his own stack of index cards. The father arrived a few minutes later. "I see that you have brought your own research," he said, smiling. "I'm curious to see what you have uncovered."

The young man wordlessly removed the top card and began to read:

Our goals can only be reached through the vehicle of a plan, in which we must fervently believe and in which we must vigorously act. There is no other route to success.

—Pablo Picasso

Obstacles are those frightful things that you see
when you take your eyes off your goals.

—Henry Ford

Find something that you are really interested in doing in your life. Pursue it, set goals, and commit yourself to excellence. Do the best you can.

—Chris Evert

My philosophy of life is that if we make up our mind what we are going to make of our lives and then work hard toward that goal, we never lose. Somehow, we win out.

—Ronald Reagan

There are really only two options regarding commitment. You're either in or you're out. There is no such thing as life in between.

—Pat Riley

Remember no effort that we make to attain
something beautiful is ever lost.

—Helen Keller

"Fantastic," said the father. "Tell me a little about how you were able to find these."

The son reflected for a moment before responding. "The concept of being goal committed seemed fairly obvious after we discussed what it was and its importance. Once I knew what I was looking for, I was amazed by what I found. There were literally thousands of quotes about goal commitment written by successful people throughout history."

"There certainly does seem to be a correlation between successful people and the way they think about goals," agreed the father. "And now that you understand goal commitment and how to identify it, we can move forward to the Second Lesson."

"That's great. What is it, and when do we start?" the young man asked enthusiastically.

The father rose from his seat and patted him on the shoulder. "Patience," he said. "I don't want you to get ahead of yourself. Meet me here in a week at the same time, and we will begin again."

The two exchanged goodbyes, and the father headed out the door to his office. The son returned to his seat and pulled his composition notebook out of his bag. He flipped it to an open page and began to write:

Key Learning Points: The First Lesson

- A large group of people have no goals or are given goals they are not passionate about by someone else.
- There is a smaller group of people who have set goals for themselves that are more like hopes and wishes.
- The smallest group of people are committed to their goals. They are specific about what they want and when they want to achieve it. They have a plan and are taking action toward their goal.
- Committing to a goal is huge because it has the power to alter your behavior and changes you from being a passive observer into a passionate participant.
- Goal-committed individuals operate differently from others. They are more focused on what they want to make happen than fearful of bad things that might happen.
- Achieving your goals is important, but the most important thing is what fully committing to your goals does for you as a person. Whether you achieve your objective or not, you never really lose when you give your best effort trying to accomplish something that is important to you. Something positive always comes out of it.

Reader Quotes

Reader Key Learning Points: The First Lesson

Reader Exercise Number One

Write a goal that you would like to commit to or have already committed to:

Write a goal-committed statement:

"I'm going to _____ (goal)
by _____ (deadline)."

List a minimum of three behavior changes or action steps that you will make immediately toward your goal:

    1.

    2.

    3.

The Second Lesson:
The Three Flavors of Hard Work

To give anything less than your best is to sacrifice the gift.
—Steve Prefontaine

The son spent the week leading up to the Second Lesson thinking about what he and the father had discussed and what he had learned. He could now easily identify goal-committed people and the different way they behaved. He could also see that they seemed more positive, productive, and quite frankly happier than people who were not. When it was finally time to meet up for the Second Lesson, the son reported to the coffee shop right on time. He was not at all surprised to see the father already there, waiting for him with a stack of index cards.

"More research?" the son asked, gesturing toward the cards.

"Of course," the father said enthusiastically, "but first tell me, how was your week?"

The son told him what he had learned by observing goal-committed people.

"Good," said the father, "but *why* do you think goal-committed individuals are more positive, productive, and happy?"

The son thought about it for a moment and then gave his

answer. "I think it is because they have a purpose, and that makes a huge difference in how they live."

The father smiled in appreciation of the young man's wisdom. "I agree," he said, "and purpose is where we will begin the Second Lesson."

"So the Second Lesson is how to have purpose?" asked the son.

"Well, not exactly," said the father. "Being goal committed gives you purpose, but having a purpose gives you the fuel you need to work hard, and that is the Second Lesson."

The young man rolled his eyes, shifted uncomfortably in his chair for a moment, and said, "I know that you told me last week that the Six Lessons are not complex, but are you really telling me that the Second Lesson is to work hard?"

"I am," said the father, "and all successful people will tell you that hard work is the key ingredient to their achievements, because nothing difficult has ever been accomplished without it."

The son sat back and folded his arms and said, "Well, that's not something I would disagree with you on; it's just that I'm afraid that this will be a very quick lesson."

"I see," said the father patiently. "And why do you think that?"

Once again, the son rolled his eyes and then impatiently blurted out, "Well, because everyone knows that you must work hard to be successful. It's not a secret; it's obvious."

"Very true. However, if you examine the thoughts of successful people, you will see that there is more to hard work than simply working hard."

"OK," the son replied skeptically, "then what is it that successful people understand about hard work that others don't?"

"Achievers instinctively know that they will need to work hard to attain their goals, as you said," the father began. "They are goal committed and fueled by purpose. This gives them the desire to work hard." The son began taking notes in his notebook as the father spoke. "They actually enjoy it; they see it as part of the process of being successful. On the other hand, less successful people often see hard work as punishment or something to be avoided at all cost."

"That's very true," said the son. "I've known many people who absolutely hated the idea of hard work. I used to think that they were just lazy, but now I'm beginning to believe that the real issue is perhaps that they lacked purpose."

The father nodded his head in appreciation of the son's insight. "Exactly," he said, "because when you are excited about your work, it doesn't seem hard at all. But when you do not have motivation, hard work can seem brutally difficult. Another thing that achievers understand about hard work is that there are different variations that are all equally important. I call them the Three Flavors of Hard Work: effort, hustle, and practice."

"Effort, hustle, and practice," repeated the son. "Aren't those all basically the same thing?"

The father shook his head. "I can see why you might think that, but they really aren't. Each is important in its own way. Effort is primarily how hard and how long you can push yourself to get the job done, and it is critical to success. Effort is the flavor most people associate with hard work because achievers understand that they cannot obtain their best results without their best efforts. Effort is the 'try hard' flavor. Hustle, on the other hand, is the art of creating good situations for yourself. It is about applying your efforts at the right time and place, as well as to the right things. Hustle is about recognizing opportunities and responding to them quickly. Hustlers have a high level of situational awareness or what we used to call street smarts. Their greatest skill is to be able to see something before anyone else and put themselves in a position to respond. Hustle is intelligent effort; it is the 'work smart' flavor." He paused briefly to take a sip of coffee and allow his words to sink in. "Practice is the simplest and yet most misunderstood of the three."

"Why do you say that?" asked the son.

"Practice is misunderstood because far too many people believe they can be good at something without practicing it. Everyone wants the glory of winning or doing something at a very high level, but very few people understand the work that goes into that. In order for you to perform at your best at anything, be it sports, music, public speaking, or a sales job, you must practice your skills consistently and with great focus. Most people do not see the value of regular practice, but it is a key component of success. Practice is the 'preparation' flavor."

"So effort, hustle, and practice are the same as trying hard, working smart, and being prepared," the son said. It was hard to argue with that logic, but the son had never really thought about hard work in those terms. He could now see how each flavor was important and how interrelated they were.

The father handed him the index cards and asked him to read them aloud. He took the cards and began:

Effort.

Success is dependent on effort.

—Sophocles

I know the price of success: dedication, hard work, and an unremitting devotion to the things you want to see happen.

—Frank Lloyd Wright

The man who can drive himself further once the effort gets painful is the man who will win.

—Roger Bannister

With slight efforts how can we achieve great results? It is foolish to even desire it.

—Euripides

There will be obstacles. There will be doubters.
There will be mistakes. But with hard work,
there are no limits.

—Michael Phelps

Without effort, you cannot be prosperous.
Though the land be good you cannot have an
abundant crop without cultivation.

—Plato

Hustle.

Things come to those who wait, but only those things left by those who hustle.

—Abraham Lincoln

Eighty percent of success is showing up.

—Woody Allen

The dream is free. The hustle is sold separately.

—Tyrese Gibson

Good things happen to those who hustle.

—Anaïs Nin

I sell ice in winter, I sell fire in hell...I'm a hustler, baby, I sell water to a well.

—Jay-Z

Without hustle, talent will only carry you so far.

—Gary Vaynerchuk

Practice.

By failing to prepare you are preparing to fail.

—Benjamin Franklin

I fear not the man who has practiced ten thousand kicks once, but I fear the man who has practiced one kick ten thousand times

—Bruce Lee

It is not the will to win, but the will to prepare to win that makes all the difference.

—Paul "Bear" Bryant

Success depends upon previous preparation, and without such preparation there is sure to be failure.

—Confucius

You've got to learn your instrument. Then you practice, practice, practice. And then, when you finally get up there on the bandstand, forget all that and just wail.

—Charlie Parker

I read an article a few years ago that said when you practice a sport a lot, you literally become a broadband. The nerve pathways in your brain contain a lot more information. As soon as you stop practicing, the pathway begins shrinking back down. Reading that changed my life. I used to wonder, why am I doing these sets? Getting onstage? Don't I know how to do this already? The answer is no. You must keep doing it. The broadband starts to narrow the moment you stop.

—Jerry Seinfeld

As the son put down the final card, he looked at the father and sheepishly admitted, "There is much more to working hard than I had considered prior to beginning the Second Lesson."

"Like many simple concepts, there is some nuance as you dig deeper," said the father. "But now it's time for you to apply some hard work of your own. Your homework will be to find six quotes on each of the three flavors."

The young man nodded, and the two agreed to meet the following morning at the same place and time. Then the son left to begin his research for the continuation of the Second Lesson.

The next day he met the father at the planned-upon time. He was excited to share the knowledge he had uncovered about effort, hustle, and practice.

"Please begin with your effort quotes," said the teacher, and his student began.

Effort.

There is no substitute for hard work.

—Thomas Edison

I've got this theory that if you give 100 percent all the time, somehow things will always work out in the end.

—Larry Bird

Enthusiasm is the mother of effort, and without
it nothing was ever accomplished.

—Ralph Waldo Emerson

A champion is someone who gets up when he can't.

—Jack Dempsey

Effort only fully releases its reward after a person refuses to quit.

—Napoleon Hill

No one who gave their best regretted it.

—George Halas

Hustle.

To improve the golden moment of opportunity and catch the good that is within our reach is the great art of life.

—William James

Opportunity dances with those who are already
on the dance floor.

—H. Jackson Brown Jr.

Mine's a pretty simple strategy: there's not a lot of talent here, but there is a lot of hustle. I have to be every place I can and be busy.

—Ryan Seacrest

What you lack in talent can be made up with desire, hustle, and giving 110 percent all the time.

—Don Zimmer

Quality is never an accident. It is always the
result of intelligent effort.

—John Ruskin

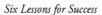
Hustle beats talent, when talent doesn't hustle.

—Ross Simmonds

Practice.

I hated every minute of training, but I said, "Don't quit." Suffer now and live the rest of your life as a champion.

—Muhammad Ali

Practice works because practice gives us a
chance to relax enough to make smart choices.

—Seth Godin

Practice does not make perfect. Only perfect practice makes perfect.

—Vince Lombardi

If I miss a day of practice, I know it. If I miss two days of practice, my manager knows it. If I miss three days of practice, my audience knows it.

—André Previn

Excellence is an art won by training and habituation. We are what we repeatedly do. Excellence, then, is not an act but a habit.

—Aristotle

After the son had put down the final card, the father asked, "What are your thoughts on hard work after completing your assignment?"

The son considered his response for a moment and then replied, "All my life I've heard people talk about hard work, but I never really spent much time thinking about what it was. I just thought that good people worked hard, and lazy people did not, and that was pretty much it. Now I am not sure there are lazy people, just people who lack purpose. When you lack purpose, it is difficult to work hard. On the other hand, the more powerful your purpose is, the less it seems like hard work." The son paused reflectively for a moment and then continued. "I also enjoyed our discussion of the different types of hard work. I think that 'flavors' are a very descriptive term, because even though we are talking about one thing, there are different ways of approaching it. Each is equally important and reliant on the others."

"How do you think the Three Flavors are related?" the father asked.

"Well, because it's only logical that in order to do your best, you must give your best effort. However, even when you are giving maximum effort, you must work intelligently and constantly be looking to give yourself the best possible chance to succeed. Finally, you must prepare yourself to be successful by practicing whatever it is that you want to be good at. So effort, hustle, and practice really are the Three Flavors of Hard Work, and each flavor is distinctly important in its own way."

"Well said," the father agreed. "I can now see that you are ready to move on to the Third Lesson. We will resume here in a week at the same time."

This annoyed the son slightly. He did not understand why the father once again wanted him to wait an entire week before beginning the next lesson. "Why is it that you only give me twenty-four hours to complete my homework, but you make me wait for a week to begin each new lesson?"

"I have my reasons," the father said, smiling. "Perhaps I will share them with you at a later time." With that he stood up and shook the son's hand. The Second Lesson had abruptly ended. The student watched him walk out the door, sighed deeply, then pulled out his composition book and began to write:

Key Learning Points: The Second Lesson

- Being goal committed gives you purpose.
- Purpose is the fuel that enables you to work hard.
- Nothing difficult has ever been accomplished without hard work.
- Achievers enjoy working hard; they see it as part of the process of being successful.
- Less successful people see hard work as punishment or something to be avoided.
- People are usually not lazy; they sometimes just lack purpose.
- The Three Flavors of Hard Work are effort, hustle and practice.
- Effort is how much you can push yourself while you are working. It is the "try hard" flavor.
- Hustle is the art of creating good situations for yourself and recognizing opportunities. It is the "work smart" flavor.
- Practice is the simplest yet most misunderstood form of hard work because most people do not value its importance. It is the "preparation" flavor.

Reader Quotes

Reader Key Learning Points

_____

_____

_____

_____

_____

_____

_____

_____

_____

_____

_____

_____

_____

_____

_____

Reader Exercise Number Two

Describe a time in your life that you put *maximum effort* into achieving a goal:

Describe a time you used *hustle* (intelligent effort) to recognize or create a positive opportunity for yourself:

Describe a situation where you committed yourself to *practice* in order to learn or perfect a skill:

The Third Lesson:
Choose the Optimal Attitude

*The longer I live, the more I realize the impact of attitude on life.
Attitude to me is more important than the past, than education,
than money, than circumstances, than failures, than successes,
than what other people think, say, or do. It is more important
than appearance, giftedness, or skill. It will make or break a
company…a church…a home. The remarkable thing is we have
a choice every day regarding the attitude we embrace for that
day. We cannot change our past…we cannot change the fact that
people will act a certain way. We cannot change the inevitable.
The only thing we can do is play the one string we have, and
that is our attitude…I am convinced that life is 10 percent what
happens to me and 90 percent how I react to it. And so it is with
you…we are all in charge of our attitudes.*
—Charles R. Swindoll

As he had done the week before, the son spent his time between lessons thinking about what he had learned. The conversation with the father reminded him of his favorite college class. It was a psychology course that he found fascinating, taught by a professor he admired a great deal. He enjoyed the class so much that he never missed a session, and he participated enthusiastically in class discussions. He met with his professor after class to ask additional questions and to inquire about upcoming assignments. He joined a study group with some of the top students in the class, and they prepared for exams together. It had not seemed like hard work at all. In fact, he was a little sad when the class ended. When he met the father at the coffee shop for the Third Lesson, he shared that story with him.

"Interesting," the father remarked, stroking his chin. "Tell me why you think that experience relates to the Three Flavors of Hard Work?"

"My purpose came from my enjoyment of the subject and my respect for the professor," the son explained. "My effort was attending every class and participating in the discussions. My hustle was getting to know my professor personally and getting additional information. My practice was surrounding myself with the brightest students in the class to do homework and prepare for my exams."

"Excellent," the father said, smiling. "I'm pleased that you have been able to identify a time in your life where your hard work led to success."

"Thank you," said the son. "But what I don't understand is why I wasn't able to do that all of the time. I would have done so much better and enjoyed school more if I had."

"Why do you think you didn't do as well in your other classes?" asked the father.

"Different reasons," said the son. "There would usually be some type of issue, either I didn't like the teacher, or I found the subject boring. Sometimes I just felt like the class was too difficult, and I didn't think I would do well."

"I'm afraid your experience is not that uncommon," said the father, "and it is also the starting point of the Third Lesson."

"I'm confused," said the son. "What do my past failures have to do with success?"

"*Everything*," the father said forcefully, "because the Third Lesson is about choosing the optimal attitude." He then leaned down and opened his briefcase, which was sitting on the floor. He reached inside and pulled out his laptop. After a few moments of setup, he pressed the screen to play a video that he had queued up. The son recognized the character Rocky Balboa played by the actor Sylvester Stallone and raised an eyebrow.

"Are we going to watch *Rocky* now, Dad? What happened to the index cards we have been reading?"

His teacher laughed and said, "Go ahead and watch this scene. We will discuss its meaning afterward."

The student watched closely as the scene began with the famous boxer talking to his own adult son.

"*Let me tell you something you already know," Rocky said. "The world ain't all sunshine and rainbows. It's a very mean and nasty place. It will beat you to your knees and keep you there permanently if you let it. You, me, or nobody is going to hit as hard as life. But it ain't about how hard you hit; it's about how hard you can get hit and keep moving forward, how much you can take and keep moving forward. That's how winning is done! Now if you know what you are worth, go out and get what you are worth. But you gotta be willing to take the hits and not go pointing fingers, saying you ain't where you want to be because of him or her or anybody. Cowards do that, and that ain't you. You're better than that!*"

As the scene faded from the screen, the father asked, "What do you think Rocky was trying to teach his son?"

The young man considered it a moment, then replied, "That life can be tough, but you have to be strong enough to take it. He is also saying that you can't blame your failures on others. You must take responsibility for yourself."

"Very true," the father agreed, "but he is also talking about the importance of choosing the optimal attitude. You see, whenever you set out to accomplish something great, you must be willing to face adversity."

"That seems like a bit of a blanket statement," replied the son. "Why would a person always have to face adversity to accomplish great things?"

"Because greatness by its very nature is difficult and rare," said the father. "If accomplishing great things were easy, everyone would do it. If everyone could do it, then the bar for greatness would increase and become more difficult yet again. So great accomplishments are always rare and difficult, which means you will need to face adversity to achieve them."

The son pondered the father's words for a moment and said, "No offense, Dad, but for a lesson on choosing the right attitude, you are kind of bumming me out. Shouldn't your message be a bit more positive?"

The father grinned good-naturedly at this. "It's not my intent to be negative, quite the opposite, in fact. Just because things get challenging does not mean they are impossible. However, you can either embrace that challenge or allow it to defeat you. What I'm trying to say is that how you choose to respond to adversity will play a huge role in whether or not you will be successful."

"I think I understand," said the son. "You are saying that having the correct attitude is our primary tool for overcoming adversity."

The father nodded his head in agreement. "Here is how it works: It is easy and natural to respond well to good news. However, whenever we experience adversity, we will have an emotional reaction. This early reaction is what I call the *Initial Negative Response* or INR. This is also completely natural and to be expected."

"What types of emotions will people having an INR experience?" asked the son.

The father paused to take a sip of coffee before answering. "Anger, fear, anxiety, jealousy, sadness, stress, or a combination of many negative emotions. The INR can be very short or last a long time depending on the individual and the level of adversity they are experiencing. At some point, however, the emotional response will begin to fade, and that is when things will become interesting."

The son was intrigued. "Why do things become interesting after the INR fades?"

"Once the initial shock and emotional reaction wear off, the individual must decide how they will respond. They will ask themselves, 'OK, now what?' and make a choice. That choice is called their attitude."

The young man considered the father's statement for a moment and then asked, "So you are saying that a person's attitude is always their choice?"

"Yes," said the father. "You don't always get to choose what happens to you or how it initially makes you feel, but ultimately it is up to you to choose how you will react to it and where you will go from there. The attitude you choose will shape your behavior, and your behavior will dictate your results."

"OK, then if our attitude is so important because it shapes our behavior and our actions, what is the difference between a good attitude and a bad attitude in your opinion?" asked the son.

The father smiled to himself; he enjoyed it when the son asked perceptive questions. "The whole concept of good and bad attitudes is where things can become a bit misleading," the older man said, "because many people feel like if they are merely positive then they have a good attitude. Others are afraid to be positive because they don't want to get their hopes up, so they adopt a negative outlook to try to protect themselves from being disappointed."

"I've done both of those things myself," admitted the son. "But isn't it better to be positive?"

"Because our attitudes directly impact our behavior it is *critical* to be positive," said the father. "It is also therefore equally important not to be negative, because negativity simply cannot create positive results." He took a sip of coffee and then continued. "But in addition to positivity and negativity, there are two less talked about concepts that have tremendous impact on our attitude: productive and unproductive mindsets."

"Isn't a positive attitude and a productive mindset basically the same thing?" the son asked.

"Your positivity has to do with your belief that you can attain your desired outcome," the father answered, "but your productivity has to do with your understanding of what you need to do and your bias toward taking action. It also determines how flexible and open you are to beneficial methods of achieving your goal." The son reflected on this thoughtfully for a moment as the father continued. "Conversely, a negative attitude consists of a low level of belief that you can attain your desired outcome. An unproductive mindset doesn't have a good understanding of what it will take, has a low action bias, and is inflexible and resistant to beneficial methods of achieving the goal." The older man then pulled out an index card with a colored diagram on it.

THE ATTITUDE MATRIX

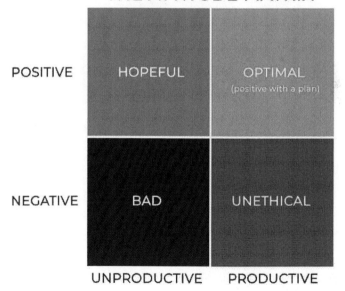

	UNPRODUCTIVE	PRODUCTIVE
POSITIVE	HOPEFUL	OPTIMAL (positive with a plan)
NEGATIVE	BAD	UNETHICAL

"This is the Attitude Matrix," he explained, pointing to the top box on the left. "Quadrant one has a high level of positivity, but the mindset is unproductive. Individuals with this type of attitude are hoping for a positive outcome but really have no idea how to make it occur. While it is always more beneficial to be positive than negative, hope is not a strategy and will only work occasionally. Quadrant two attitudes are high in both positivity and productivity. They believe that the goal will be accomplished, and they have a good understanding of what will be required. Quadrant two attitudes are the most likely of all to succeed because they are *positive with a plan*. It is the combination of positivity with productivity that creates the optimal attitude." He pointed to the bottom-left square. "Quadrant three attitudes, however, are both negative and unproductive. They have a low level of belief that the goal can be accomplished and no idea how to make it occur. This is the classic 'bad attitude.' Individuals with this type of attitude have no chance of succeeding."

The son studied the attitude matrix for a moment and then asked, "What about quadrant four? What is the unethical attitude?"

"Occasionally, we find individuals who possess high levels of negativity but also possess high levels of productivity. This combination creates a desperate win-at-any-cost mentality. Quadrant four is where we see unethical approaches to achieving goals. It's important to understand that goals achieved in this manner are often short-lived, and people who take this route often suffer disastrous consequences in the long term."

The younger man silently evaluated the attitude matrix for

a moment and then said, "So what you are saying is that if you want a positive outcome, you must always choose a positive attitude, because positive outcomes don't come from negative attitudes. In addition, the more productive your outlook is, the more realistic attaining your goal will become."

"Precisely," said the father as he pulled the stack of index cards out of his briefcase and handed them to the son. "You must be *positive with a plan*."

The son took the cards and began to read:

I never saw a pessimistic general win a battle.

—Dwight Eisenhower

Our attitudes control our lives. Attitudes are a secret power working twenty-four hours a day for good or bad. It is of paramount importance that we know how to harness and control this great force.

—Irving Berlin

We must accept finite disappointment, but
never lose infinite hope.

—Martin Luther King

Every morning you have a choice. Are you going to be a positive thinker or a negative thinker? Positive thinking will energize you.

—Jon Gordon

Positive thinking will let you do everything
better than negative thinking will.

—Zig Ziglar

I've missed over nine thousand shots in my career. I've lost almost three hundred games. Twenty-six times I've been trusted to take the game-winning shot, and I have missed. I failed over and over again in my life, and that is why I succeed.

—Michael Jordan

As the son put down the final card, he asked the father, "See you here at the same time tomorrow?" The father nodded his agreement, and with that the two men shook hands and parted company.

The following day they arrived at the same time. They ordered coffee, and when it was prepared, they sat at their usual table. "I'm excited to share my attitude quotes," said the son. "It must be an incredibly important topic because I had a hard time picking just six. I could have selected ten times as many."

The father smiled at the son's enthusiasm. "Great to see that you have such a good attitude about your attitude quotes," he deadpanned. "Please share what you have found."

The son groaned, rolled his eyes at this "dad joke," and then began:

You cannot have a positive life and a negative mind.

—Joyce Meyer

For success, attitude is equally as important as ability.

—Walter Scott

We may encounter many defeats, but we must not be defeated.

—Maya Angelou

I think whether you are having setbacks or not, the role of a leader is to always display a winning attitude.

—Colin Powell

I am an optimist. It does not seem to be too much use being anything else.

—Winston Churchill

We who lived in the concentration camps can remember the men who walked through the huts comforting others, giving away their last piece of bread. They may have been few in number, but they offer sufficient proof that everything can be taken from a man but one thing: the last of the human freedoms... to choose one's attitude in any given set of circumstances.

—Viktor E. Frankl

After the son finished his final quote, he could see that the father was deeply moved. The two men sat in a comfortable silence as each reflected upon the enormous power of choosing the right attitude. After a few moments, the younger man spoke. "I know that my assignment was to bring six quotes about attitude that have meaning for me, but I found one additional thing that I would like to share." With a look of mildly pleased surprise, the father nodded his approval. "It's the poem 'If' by Rudyard Kipling."

He then took a sheet of paper from his notebook and began to read:

If you can keep your head when all about you are losing theirs and blaming it on you, if you can trust yourself when all men doubt you, but make allowance for their doubting too; if you can wait and not be tired by waiting, or being lied about, don't deal in lies, or being hated, don't give way to hating, and yet don't look too good or talk to wise.

If you can dream—and not make dreams your master; if you can think—and not make thoughts your aim; if you can meet triumph and disaster and treat those impostors just the same; if you can bear to hear the truth you've spoken twisted by naves to make a trap for fools, or watch the things you gave your life to, broken, and stoop to build 'em up with worn-out tools.

If you can make one heap of all your winnings and risk it all on one turn of pitch-and-toss, and lose, and start again at your beginnings and never breathe a word about your loss; if you can force your heart and nerve and sinew to serve your turn long after they are gone, and so hold on when there is nothing in you except the will which says to them: 'Hold on!'

If you can talk with crowds and keep your virtue, or walk with Kings—nor lose the common touch, if neither foes nor loving friends can hurt you, if all men count with you, but none too much; if you can fill the unforgiving minute with sixty seconds' worth of distance run, yours is the earth and everything that's in it, and—which is more—you'll be a man, my son!

As the son finished his reading, the father looked at him. He was astonished by his progress over the past month. It was clear to him that his student was quickly able to grasp the concepts contained within the Six Lessons and validate them for himself. "That was a great addition to your attitude quotes," the father said. "What made you want to share it with me?"

The son thought about it for a moment and replied, "I love the name 'If' and that the poem is a parent teaching a child that he can take on any challenge if he has the right attitude. I plan on keeping a copy of it where I can see it as a reminder of the importance of choosing the optimal attitude."

The father smiled and said nothing. He had learned from experience that the best teachers understand the correct moment to end each lesson. He shook the son's hand and gave him a pat on the back. "Well said. I will see you back here in a week," he called over his shoulder as he left the coffee shop.

After the older man had exited, the son pulled out his notebook and began to record what he had learned. He wrote:

Key Learning Points: The Third Lesson

- Do not expect great accomplishments to be easy. Great things by their very nature are difficult and rare.
- You must expect some adversity anytime you attempt to achieve a worthwhile goal.
- The attitude you choose is your number-one tool to overcome adversity.
- Anyone can react well when positive things happen.
- When negative things happen, it is natural to experience an *Initial Negative Response.*
- Once the INR subsides, you will choose one of four attitudes: hopeful, optimal, bad, or unethical.
- A positive outlook with an unproductive mindset is a hopeful attitude. While it is important to be positive, hope is not a strategy and will only succeed occasionally.
- A positive outlook with a productive mindset is the optimal attitude and gives you the best chance of being successful because you are *positive with a plan.*
- A negative outlook with an unproductive mindset is the classic "bad attitude" and has no chance at being successful.
- A negative outlook with a productive mindset creates a win-at-all-cost mentality. This is where we see unethical approaches to achieving goals, often with catastrophic results.

- An individual may not be able to control what happens to them or how it makes them feel initially, but they always have the ability to choose their attitude.

Reader Quotes

Reader Key Learning Points

_____

_____

_____

_____

_____

_____

_____

_____

_____

_____

_____

_____

_____

_____

_____

Reader Exercise Number Three

On a scale of one to ten, how positive do you consider yourself to be most of the time?

Now list six people, things, or events in your life that you are *grateful* for and why.

Describe your feelings after listing what you are grateful for. Does being grateful impact your positivity?

The Fourth Lesson:
Surround Yourself with Talent

The quality of your life is the quality of your relationships.
—Tony Robbins

After the Third Lesson, the son began to notice a big difference in his own outlook. While he had always believed that a positive attitude was important, he had not spent a lot of time considering the importance of having a productive mindset. He decided he would look up the definition of the word productive in the dictionary. It said:

Productive: 1. Having the power of producing; generative; creative. 2. Producing readily or abundantly; fertile. 3. Causing or bringing about.

He now understood that it was not enough to simply be positive. You must have the idea of how you are going to make things happen and be open to good new ideas as well. He supposed choosing the optimal attitude was very similar to the First Lesson of committing to goals. He now fully believed that attitude was a choice and that the optimal attitude for success is a high level of belief that you will succeed and a good idea of how you plan to make it happen; you needed to be positive with a plan. But there was something troubling him about that statement. What if a person was committed to a goal and had a positive attitude but had no idea how to be productive and come up with a plan to accomplish it? Would they always be stuck in the hopeful attitude quadrant? If they lost hope, would they become discouraged and slip into negativity and develop a bad attitude? Could they become so desperate that they fall into the unethical quadrant and attempt to cheat, take advantage of someone, or even break the law? While he did not approve of any of those outcomes, the realist in him could see how they could easily happen. He decided that he would pose the question of how to add a productive mindset to a positive attitude when he met with the father for the Fourth Lesson.

He got to the coffee shop early on the appointed day, and after the father had arrived and settled in, the son said, "I've been thinking quite a bit about the importance of choosing an attitude that is both positive and productive. It seems obvious to me that a positive outlook is something that each person must choose for themselves. What I'm less clear on is how to find productivity. If it's not something I understand, how will I figure it out?"

If the father was surprised by the son's question, he certainly did not show it. In fact, the son thought he could detect a faint smile on the older man's face, almost as if he had been expecting to be asked that. "You are correct," the father replied. "A positive outlook is something you give to yourself. However, a productive mindset may require knowledge or skills that you do not possess." He paused to take a sip of coffee before continuing. "However, you can sometimes get the information that you need from other people, and that is the starting point of the Fourth Lesson."

"So the Fourth Lesson is to learn from others?" asked the son.

The father studied the son's face calmly for a moment and then responded. "The Fourth Lesson is that you must surround yourself with talent if you wish to improve your productivity."

"I've never heard that before," said the son. "What exactly does that mean, and why is it important?"

The teacher had anticipated the student's question and began his answer. "Surrounding yourself with talent is critical for success because, whether we admit it or not, each of us is influenced by others to varying degrees."

The son considered this comment for a moment and said, "I'm not sure that I agree with that. Aren't we all ultimately responsible for our own actions?"

"Yes, that's true," the father agreed. "Everyone is responsible for their own actions; however, those actions are bound to be influenced in some way by others. That is why it is so important to choose whom we associate with wisely if we want to improve our productivity."

"I think I see what you are saying," said the son. "If we are going to be influenced by the people around us, we should choose to be around people who can influence us productively and in the direction of our goals. But is that always possible?"

"It can be challenging," the father conceded, "but it is critical to find talented people who live their lives in a way that has a positive impact on us while at the same time eliminating relationships that are harmful to us."

"That would seem easier said than done," said the son, "and how will I recognize the type of person who is talented in the way you are describing?"

"Excellent question," said the father. "Let me begin by describing the six types of talent you need to look for in people who will help you to improve your productivity. I call them the Six C's of Talent: coaching talent, consulting talent, complementary talent, competitive talent, connecting talent, and caring talent."

The young man began taking notes in his notebook as the father continued. "The first C is coaching talent, and it is absolutely critical to success. Coaches are people with skills they can teach us and can give constructive feedback on our development. Good coaches can objectively evaluate our strengths and weaknesses and can help us develop strategies to improve our productivity."

"I've always thought of coaches as people with clipboards and whistles who do a lot of yelling," the son said with a laugh.

"The athletic coach is one type," the father admitted, "but coaches come in many forms. For example, teachers, managers, and advisers can all be coaches. The thing that all true coaches have in common is that they can help you get better at something, and they want to see you win. If they don't have both of those qualities, they cannot be your coach."

"Understood," said the son. "Tell me about the next type of talent I should look for."

"The second C is consulting talent," said the father. "Consulting talent is similar to coaching talent, but there are key differences between coaches and consultants. Consultants have valuable information that they can share with us about how to improve, but they are not able to give us direct, ongoing feedback the way a coach can. In order to work effectively with a consultant, you must proactively seek their information, understand it, and apply it to your own situations. Authors, speakers, bloggers, and podcasters are all forms of consulting talent."

"So the difference is that I would actually know a coach but I might not have a direct or personal relationship with a consultant?"

"Precisely," said the father. "It may be impractical for you to have a relationship with a famous expert, but they may possess fantastic information that can really help you improve. The great news is that libraries, bookstores, and websites are full of outstanding consultants; therefore, it is very easy to surround yourself with this type of talent." The father gave the son some time to finish his notes before continuing.

"The third C is complementary talent. These are individuals who possess strengths that you don't have or that combine nicely with the talents that you do have."

"I get it," said the son. "Your talents literally complement each other, so that together, you can accomplish more."

"Exactly," said the father. "People with complementary talents bring out the best in each other, like Lennon and McCartney, Kobe and Shaq, or Steve Jobs and Steve Wozniak. People with complementary talents are, in fact, teammates."

"Do people with complementary talents always get along personally?" asked the son.

"I would say generally yes, but not always. In the context we are discussing, the focus is on the results that you achieve with the other person, not necessarily the personal relationship."

"Interesting," said the son. "That brings us to the Fourth C. What is that?"

"Competitive talent," said the father. "These are talented people who are trying to achieve the same goals that you are. In some cases, they may actually be more skilled than you, or they are actively trying to defeat you."

"Wait a minute," the son protested. "Why would I want to associate myself with someone who was trying to beat me?"

"It does seem counterintuitive, I suppose," mused the father, "but it's all about your perspective. Many of the greatest accomplishments of mankind were the result of fierce competition between talented rivals. Great artists have been inspired by the works of talented contemporaries; great athletes have been pushed beyond their perceived limits by outstanding competition."

"Can you give me some examples?" asked the son.

"Of course," said the father. "The United States put a man on the moon as a direct response to the Soviet space program, both Van Gogh and Monet inspired each other creatively, and, as a child, Tiger Woods dreamed of surpassing Jack Nicklaus's golfing records. Having a competitive challenge can be very positive."

"I see what you mean," said the son. "It is all about perspective and that having someone to push you isn't necessarily a bad thing."

"The next type of talent is what I call connecting talent.

Connectors are people in our lives that can help us find people and opportunities that are positive for us. They may not have the information we need, but they know how to help us find it."

The son nodded his head in agreement. He had often marveled at people who seemed to know everyone and were able to connect themselves and others to good situations. He had to admit that he had never seen it as a talent before, but it was easy to see the value of associating with people who were connectors.

"Let's see," the son said, looking at his notes, "we've covered coaching, consulting, complementary, competitive, and connecting talent. That is five types. What is the sixth and final C?"

"Caring talent," stated the father. "While other types of talent are not necessarily about personal relationships, caring talent is 100 percent about being a part of a supportive personal relationship. Coaches teach skills and give us feedback, we learn from the teachings and experience of consultants, competitors sharpen our focus, and people who have talents that are complementary are teammates who can help us accomplish more. Connectors may not have the talent or information we need, but they can help us find it. Caring talent is completely different, however, because people with caring talent are only interested in supporting us and nurturing our aspirations."

"I can understand why people with caring talent are important," said the son, "because they can help you feel good about yourself and support you. But I can also see how that might not be a good thing, if it is taken to the extreme."

"True," said the father, "because if a person only surrounds themselves with caring talent, they can become somewhat sheltered and get a false sense of reality. While we all need encouragement and people who are in our corner no matter what, it is important that we recognize those relationships for what they are and not become overly reliant on them."

The son listened intently. The different types of talent seemed very distinct to him now that the father had identified each of them.

"So the underlying factor is that talented people can contribute to us in a variety of ways," said the son. "But what about people who don't make us better or contribute to our growth?"

The older man evaluated the son's question for a moment before answering. "It is possible to have relationships that are neutral and neither help nor harm you in any way. However, it is essential that you eliminate relationships that are negative or destructive. So, for example, no type of physical or emotional abuse, chemical addiction, or any type of destructive behavior can be a part of your life if you wish to achieve your maximum potential."

The son considered this advice thoughtfully for a moment and then asked, "Can you tell me the difference between tough coaching and abuse?"

"That is a great question, because sometimes coaches need to give us very direct feedback that can be difficult to hear in order to improve our performance. I would say then that it is necessary to go back to the requirements of being a coach. They must have a skill that they can teach you, and they must want you to succeed. If they do not have those two qualities, they are just giving you a hard time. True coaches do not get personal with their feedback, and they never get physical, so anytime there is name-calling, insults, physical abuse, or intimidation, it is no longer coaching, and it is a situation you need to get yourself out of."

"I can certainly see your point about eliminating negative relationships," said the son, "but what about your earlier point regarding addicted people? Don't they deserve our help?"

"Perhaps," said the father, "if they have an issue they're trying to change or they are in active recovery, they certainly deserve our support. In fact, people who are in recovery are practicing goal-committed behavior, and that is a very positive thing. On the other hand, if someone has an addiction, they are not committed to changing, their future is in serious jeopardy, and you won't be able to help them until they decide to commit to recovery."

The son processed this statement for a moment and then asked, "So what you are saying is that I can only help people who are trying to help themselves?"

"Remember," said the father, "motivation comes from within, and inspiration comes from others. You cannot motivate someone who is unmotivated, but you can inspire them through your own actions and decisions."

The two men were quiet for a moment as they reflected on the conversation. The older man then reached into his pocket and pulled out the index cards he had prepared for the Fourth Lesson. He handed them to the son who, at this point, understood what was expected of him.

He took the first card and began reading aloud:

Surround yourself only with people who are going to lift you higher.

—Oprah Winfrey

I think it is counterproductive in many ways to pretend you know things that you really don't. You surround yourself with people who are the real experts.

—Mario Andretti

When I was a kid, there was no collaboration;
it's you with a camera bossing your friends
around. But as an adult, filmmaking is all about
appreciating the talents of the people you
surround yourself with and knowing you could
never have made any of these films by yourself.

—Steven Spielberg

It's very important to surround yourself with
people you can learn from.

—Reba McEntire

Surround yourself with good people. People that are going to be honest with you and look after your best interest.

—Derek Jeter

Show me your friends, and I'll show you your future.

—Dan Peña

The son put down the last card. "I know that you are going to want me to go and find my own quotes about surrounding myself with talent, and you will want me here tomorrow, but I have a question for you first."

"What would you like to know?" the father asked.

"Why do I need to find my own quotes, and why do I need to always find them by the next day?"

The father smiled thoughtfully before replying. "It is important for you to find your own quotes because this is your journey, not mine. Only you can decide what is meaningful to you. The reason I ask you to get them in twenty-four hours is because I want to teach you to take immediate action on the things that are important to you."

"If that is the case, then why do we always wait a week before we can move on to the next lesson?" the son asked.

"Because I want you to take what you have learned into the world and observe it," said the father, "so you can think about it and see for yourself that it is true."

The son nodded. Now that he had this insight, he better understood the father's method of teaching. "I get your point," he said. "See you here tomorrow at the same time then?"

"I will be waiting," the father said as he watched the son walk out of the coffee shop to begin his research.

The following day, however, the pair arrived at the same time. They greeted each other cordially and ordered coffee. After each was seated with a steaming cup, the son pulled out his index cards and began to read:

"I'm indebted to my father for living, but I'm indebted to my teacher for living well.

—Alexander the Great

I'm not the smartest fellow in the room, but I can sure pick smart colleagues.

—Franklin D. Roosevelt

Fire the villains in your life.

—Heather Monahan

If you want to get healthy, you must surround yourself with a group of people who are getting healthy, and you have to connect yourself to a community that is doing what you want to do.

—Henry Cloud

None of us is as smart as all of us.

—Ken Blanchard

I have the best people around me. None of them has ever been on the radio. They're all such great people, and I found that I was able to be a better person when I was doing the radio show. It kept me from being a radio person.

—Bobby Bones

As the son put down the last card, he looked at the father and said, "Before beginning the Fourth Lesson, I thought that great people did not need the help of others, but now I understand that part of the secret to their success are the talents of the people whom they surround themselves with. That's how they can have attitudes that are both positive and productive."

"So many talented people fail to reach their potential because they never put themselves in a position to be coached, developed, pushed, or encouraged," said the father. "Others are afraid to ask for help and think they must do it all on their own."

"I agree with all that," said the son. "However, the difference in what you are saying is that you are putting the responsibility on the shoulders of the individual to go out and find talented people to surround themselves with, not to just sit around and wait for them to show up in your life."

The father raised an eyebrow and gave the son a long look. "You understand," he said knowingly, "which means you are now ready for the Fifth Lesson." The older man then reached into his briefcase and pulled out yet another index card. On it the Six C's were listed and broken down in the following manner:

SIX C's OF TALENT

COACHING & **C**ONSULTING	>	**DEVELOP SKILLS**
COMPLEMENTARY & **C**OMPETITIVE	>	**SHARPEN SKILLS**
CONNECTING & **C**ARING	>	**NURTURE SKILLS**

The son accepted the card and placed it in his notebook. "I suppose, then, I will see you in a week," he said, smiling. "Same time and place."

The father shook the son's hand, stood, and headed off to work as the younger man prepared to begin recording his key learning points from the Fourth Lesson. After discussing it with the father, he now understood the importance of acting quickly on things that were important to him. Besides, he reasoned, what better time to do it than now with the lesson fresh in his mind? He put his pen to the paper and began to write:

Key Learning Points: The Fourth Lesson

- When we surround ourselves with talented people, we improve our ability to become productive.
- While we are all ultimately responsible for our own actions, we cannot help but to be influenced by our associates.
- Whenever possible we need to make the choice to be around people who positively influence us toward our goals.
- We need to eliminate or minimize relationships that are harmful to us.
- Coaching talent: people who can teach us a skill, give us feedback on how to improve, and want to see us win.
- Consulting talent: people who are experts in a field that we are trying to improve in. We take their knowledge and try to apply it to our own life whether we get to meet them or not.
- Complementary talent: teammates who have talents we do not have or that combine nicely with our talents, so that together we may achieve more.
- Competitive talent: while it may seem counterintuitive, many times a talented rival can help us improve by sharpening our focus.
- Connecting talent: people who may not have the information or skill that we need but can help us find it.
- Caring talent: people in our lives who care about our

well-being and nurture our aspirations. While these relationships help us feel good about ourselves, we must recognize that they will not always improve our skill or performance.

- Coaches sometimes must give us difficult feedback; however, great coaches never make it personal, abusive, or get physical.

- It is up to each individual to find talented people who can help them. You cannot just wait for them to show up in your life.

Reader Quotes

_____

_____

_____

_____

_____

_____

_____

_____

_____

_____

_____

_____

_____

_____

_____

_____

Reader Key Learning Points

_____

_____

_____

_____

_____

_____

_____

_____

_____

_____

_____

_____

_____

_____

_____

_____

Reader Exercise Number Four

Who in your life is a coach for you?

What consultants do you follow?

Who has talents that complement yours?

Who provides you with positive competition?

Who in your life is a connector?

Who in your life supports you in a caring way?

The Fifth Lesson:
Exit the Comfort Zone

I want to stand close to the edge without going over. Out on the edge you can see all kinds of things you can't see from the middle.
—Kurt Vonnegut

The son met the father for the beginning of the Fifth Lesson. They greeted each other warmly. The son had noticed that, as the process of the Six Lessons unfolded, he looked forward to connecting with his dad more and more. He could tell that the "teacher" was enjoying their talks as well. Per the father's method, he had spent the week thinking about the previous lesson of surrounding himself with talent. He could really see how adding talented people to his life while eliminating negative relationships could have a powerful impact.

It makes perfect sense, he thought. *Surrounding myself with good, strong people can only make me better.* While he had no doubts about it, he did have one nagging thought that continued to return to him. *What is my role in all of this?* he wondered. *Talented people in my life will help me, but what am I doing to improve myself?*

He asked that very question of the father when they had

both had their coffee and were seated at the table. The father responded by showing him a diagram on a spare index card. It was a small circle surrounded by a larger one. Inside the small circle was the word "comfort." Outside the larger circle was the word "panic."

"This inside circle represents a person's comfort zone," the father said. "The comfort zone is a small, safe place with minimal risk and predictable outcomes. However, the trade-off for that safety is that no personal growth or development can take place in the comfort zone."

The son nodded his head as the father continued. "Outside the larger circle is the panic zone. It is a dangerous place where bad decisions and desperate actions happen. Psychologists often refer to this as the fight-or-flight response. Very little development occurs in the panic zone because very little thought goes into actions that occur when people are panicked."

The son studied the diagram for a moment and asked,

"What about the space between the comfort zone and the panic zone?"

The father smiled. "I was hoping you would notice that," he said.

He then took the card and wrote two words in the space between the comfort zone and the panic zone. "The space that you are referring to is called the learning zone, and it is the area where all personal improvement occurs. The farther a person can push themselves out of their comfort zone without slipping into the panic zone, the greater their development."

"So the Fifth Lesson is to push myself outside the comfort zone?" asked the son.

"Yes. It is understanding that you must exit the comfort zone if you wish to grow."

The two men pondered this concept while they sipped their

coffee. Eventually the son spoke. "I can see what you are saying," he said. "How will I ever learn and improve if I am unwilling to try new things that are beyond me?"

The father nodded his head in agreement. "Allow me to share with you what I call the Four Laws of Learning," he said. He reached into his back pocket and pulled out his wallet. He opened it and pulled out what appeared to be a very old slip of paper, which he unfolded and read to the son:

FOUR LAWS OF LEARNING

1 Learning offers the only true path to personal development.

2 Learning keeps us in a state of perpetual growth.

3 The absence of learning limits options and can create boredom and negativity.

4 The presence of learning increases options and can stimulate creativity and positivity.

The father folded the paper and put it back in his wallet. "I keep these with me as a reminder to myself anytime I get anxious about trying something new," he stated. "The Four Laws help me remember that I need to get out of my comfort zone."

"That's cool," said the son, "but I also know many people who don't like learning."

The father disagreed. "Well, it's not so much that they don't enjoy learning as much as it is that they prefer to be comfortable, because learning creates challenge and introduces the possibility of failure. Some individuals' fear of failure is greater than their desire to grow."

"Ah, I see," said the son. "If your fear of failure is greater than your desire to grow, you will never leave the comfort zone."

The father said nothing but nodded his head thoughtfully. The son now understood that when the father responded that way, the older man felt that the point had been made and nothing more needed to be added.

The father then reached into his case and retrieved the quotes he had prepared for the Fifth Lesson. He handed them to the son who began to read:

I am always doing what I cannot do yet in order
to learn how to do it.

—Vincent van Gogh

Even the genius asks his questions.

—Tupac Shakur

All progress takes place outside the comfort zone.

—Michael John Bobak

If you aren't in over your head, how do you
know how tall you are?

—T. S. Eliot

Life begins at the end of your comfort zone.

—Neale Donald Walsch

The capacity to learn is a gift; the ability to learn
is a skill; the willingness to learn is a choice.

—Brian Herbert

As the son put down the final card, he looked slightly discouraged. "This is something I have always struggled with," he admitted.

The father nodded his head sympathetically. "Honestly, many people do struggle with it, so you are not alone."

"Why do you think so many people have difficulty leaving their comfort zone?" the son asked.

The father reflected for a moment. "I think it is because the human mind is wired to try to keep us comfortable and safe. Getting out of your comfort zone is a conscious choice that takes some courage and the willingness to be uncomfortable."

"If I want to be my best self, it's a step I must be willing to take," said the son. "I must be willing to do things that others are unwilling to do."

"You must become comfortable with the idea of feeling uncomfortable," the father said.

The son finished his coffee, said goodbye, and headed out the door to begin his research. He looked down at the card the teacher had given him with a picture of the comfort zone, panic zone, and learning zone. Visualizing the zones helped him tremendously. *Not comfort or panic,* he said to himself. *I want to stay in the learning zone.*

The next morning, the son arrived a few minutes after the father. Once he had gotten his coffee and taken his seat, he reached into his backpack, pulled out his comfort zone quotes, and began to read:

In any given moment we have two options:
to step forward into growth or step back into
safety.

—Abraham Maslow

Too many of us are not living our dreams
because we are living our fears.

—Les Brown

I learned to take on things I had never done before. Growth and comfort do not coexist.

—Virginia Rometty

Adventure should be 80 percent 'I think this is manageable' but it's good to have that last 20 percent where you are right outside your comfort zone. Still safe but outside your comfort zone.

—Bear Grylls

One of the most fascinating lessons I've absorbed about life is that the struggle is good.

—Joe Rogan

The man who does not read has no advantage over the man who can't.

—Mark Twain

You will always miss 100 percent of the shots
you don't take.

—Wayne Gretzky

If you push through that feeling of being scared, that feeling of taking a risk, really amazing things can happen.

—Marissa Mayer

No amount of security is worth the suffering of a mediocre life chained to the routine that has killed your dreams.

—Maya Mendoza

The biggest risk is not taking any risk. In a world that's changing really quickly, the only strategy that is guaranteed to fail is not taking risks.

—Mark Zuckerberg

Our doubts are traitors, and make us lose the good we oft might win, by fearing to attempt.

—William Shakespeare

As the son finished reading, the father seemed puzzled. "Great job on finding the quotes," the father said. "But I'm curious. I only ask for six. Why did you do more?"

"I did more as a statement to myself," the son said, "to show that I'm taking charge of my own learning. As a result I decided that I would keep researching until I was satisfied and not be locked into a set number."

The father nodded with pride. "Doing that was a small victory. If you apply this approach to each day, you will find your accomplishments will begin to multiply. Just imagine what the world would be like if everyone took responsibility for their own learning and pushed through their comfort zone."

The son smiled. He could tell by the older man's tone that he had mastered the Fifth Lesson and there would be no further teaching. The pair made small talk while they finished their coffee and made plans to meet the following week.

After the father said goodbye and headed out of the shop, the son pulled out his notebook to record his key learning points.

Key Learning Points: The Fifth Lesson

- No growth occurs in the comfort zone.
- Bad decisions and fight or flight occur in the panic zone.
- The learning zone is outside of the comfort zone but not in the panic zone. It is where almost all personal development happens.
- If your fear of failure is greater than your desire to grow, you will stay in your comfort zone.
- Successful people are comfortable with the idea of being uncomfortable. They recognize that they need to take responsibility for their own learning and exit the comfort zone.

The Four Laws of Learning
- Learning offers the only true path to self-improvement.
- Learning keeps us in a state of perpetual growth.
- The absence of learning limits options and can create boredom and negativity.
- The presence of learning increases options and can stimulate creativity and positivity.

Reader quotes

Reader Key Learning Points

_____

_____

_____

_____

_____

_____

_____

_____

_____

_____

_____

_____

_____

_____

_____

_____

Reader Exercise Number Five

Describe an area of your life where you feel that you are stuck or caught in a comfort zone.

What impact do you feel that it is having on your personal growth?

What risks are you taking by staying in your comfort zone?

What risks would you be taking by exiting your comfort zone?

List a minimum of three actions you could take that would help you break out of your comfort zone.

The Sixth Lesson:
The Golden Triangle

Health is a state of complete harmony of the body, mind, and spirit.

—B.K.S. Iyengar

The son spent the week between the Fifth and Sixth Lessons trying to find ways to stay in his learning zone and out of his comfort zone. While he had initially not cared much for the idea of taking a week between lessons, now that he understood the purpose, he actually enjoyed it. He realized it gave him the time to process and apply what he had learned to his own life. When the father met him at the coffee shop later the following week, the son told him about his change of heart and how he had begun to value the extra time.

"What is it about the extra time that you appreciate?" the father asked.

The son paused for a moment and then said, "I suppose that it's because it gives me the time to consider things. It makes me feel like I'm sorting things out and thinking about getting better."

"That's important," said the father. "Self-development and

becoming the best version of yourself is a major part of becoming successful. It gives you the best possible chance to succeed."

The son nodded in agreement. "Understood," he said, "and I would bet that the Sixth Lesson has something to do with becoming the best version of yourself."

The father suppressed a smile. He had forgotten how intuitive the son could be. He had to admit that, despite their difficult past, the young man was one of his favorite students.

"The Sixth Lesson," he began, "is about finding the Golden Triangle. Any idea what that means?"

The son pondered the question and considered guessing but decided against it. "No idea," he said. "I've never heard of the Golden Triangle. What is it?"

The older man took a sip of coffee before beginning his description: "For thousands of years, people have talked about the importance of the relationship between the body, mind, and values in successful living." He then produced an index card with a symbol drawn on it.

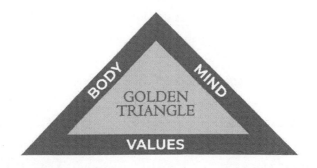

The son evaluated the picture of the triangle as the father

continued. "Let's discuss each of the sides of the triangle and why they are important." The student leaned forward, giving the teacher his undivided attention. "We will start with the body, because in a very real sense, the body is the vehicle through which we live our lives. It is critical that we improve ourselves physically and take care of our health if we are to be at our best."

"I don't disagree with you on that per se, but I can see how some people might view that as shallow or superficial," the son observed.

The father chuckled in response. "We do live in a society that places a huge value on appearance; however, I am not referring to the body in only superficial terms. While most of us will not be confused with a professional athlete or be on the cover of a magazine, we each have a personal-best body that we can attain at any age. Part of being your best as a person is trying to be at your best physically, whatever that means to you."

"I see what you are saying," said the son. "Rather than allowing someone else tell you what you should be, it's OK to set your own physical standard and try to reach it."

"Exactly," the father confirmed. "By working on improving our health and fitness, we accomplish many things. When we exercise, eat right, and get enough sleep, we are tangibly increasing the potential of our performance. In addition, the healthier our bodies are, the higher the quality of our lives will be. Finally, all of our other systems, including our thinking, work better when we are physically healthy."

"I love that," the son added, "especially the part about the healthy body-mind connection."

"Yes, the mind is also a muscle," the father said. "It requires positive fuel, exercise, and training to keep it strong. We must read, learn, and get out of our mental comfort zone if we are to keep the mind functioning at its highest level."

"So you are saying that we need to not only stimulate our bodies with exercise, but we have to stimulate our mind by constantly using it? What exactly does that accomplish?"

"You must understand," said the father, "that successful people are lifelong learners. They do not get to a certain point and then stop. They understand that the mind is basically an *input-impacts-output system*. They believe that if they quit learning, they quit growing. If you feed your mind negative thoughts and the equivalent of mental junk food, or you do not exercise it on a daily basis, it will not function at its full capacity. However, the good news is that if you do use it and stimulate it with high-quality mental activity and positive thoughts, your mind will become stronger."

"What exactly do you mean that the mind is an input-impacts-output system?" the son queried.

The father paused for a moment before giving his answer. "What I mean is that you must keep learning, and you must be very conscious of your self-talk and the content you process because you will create positive or negative results based on your thoughts."

"So what you are saying," the son asked, "is that it is important to monitor my thinking because my thoughts will impact my actions? But is that really possible? Aren't my thoughts just thoughts?"

"Thoughts and ideas are extremely powerful, because whatever you focus on expands," the father replied. "If you focus on positivity, you will get positive outcomes; if you focus on negativity, that is what will happen."

"My thoughts control my attitude, and my attitude impacts the results I will achieve," said the son. "I understand."

The father nodded his head in agreement. "Your body is the vehicle; your mind is the engine."

The younger man considered that analogy for a moment and then asked, "So if that is the case, what is the values side of the triangle?"

The father took a sip of his coffee before answering. "The values portion of the Golden Triangle is your guidance system. Contained in it are your core beliefs that allow you to tell what is right and what is wrong."

The son reflected on the father's answer for a moment and then asked, "I see many types of people who all have different ideas about what is right and what is wrong. How do you justify that?"

"It is true. Not all core beliefs are the same, so not everyone shares the same values," the father replied. "However, that fact is less important than each individual knowing and understanding their own value system."

"Why do you say that?"

"Because despite differences in values, there are two distinct reasons why it is important for each of us to have solid core beliefs that are based in principle. The first is to give us guidance on the decisions we are faced with in our daily lives."

"I see what you mean," the son said. "Sometimes when an individual is faced with a difficult choice, they need guidance, and solid core beliefs would help them make the best decision."

"Correct," agreed the father. "The second reason it is important to have a core belief system is to help guide us back on track when our judgment fails and we do the wrong thing."

"Wait a minute," protested the son. "I thought the entire point of a guidance system was to keep us from making mistakes."

"It is," the father said, reassuring him. "But people are imperfect and often make poor choices. When that inevitably happens, having a core belief system helps them get back on track."

"Sort of like a road map," said the son, "so that if you make a wrong turn, you can still find your way home."

"Exactly right," said the father. "This road map contains the values that drive our decisions."

"What happens when people don't follow their core values or, even worse, create artificial values that lack integrity?"

"That does happen, but the farther a person drifts from their core values, the more unfulfilled they will be," the father said. "Most won't be successful, but even if they are able to achieve success, they will be conflicted. You can mislead others sometimes, but ultimately, you will never fool yourself. You cannot become the best version of yourself in this manner."

"I believe that," the son said, "because people who live in harmony with their core values have a huge advantage. They can focus all of their energy on what they're doing and feel positive about it."

"A very good point," said the father as he produced the index cards for the Sixth Lesson and handed them to the son. "Please read these aloud starting with the quotes on the body."

The son began to read:

Body.

The body never lies.

—Martha Graham

Having the body you want begins with loving the body you have.

—Mandy Ingber

We employed the mind to rule, the body to serve.

—Sallust

It is the mind that makes the body.

—Sojourner Truth

The successful men I have admired all built
their bodies.

—Dwayne Johnson

There is more wisdom in your body than in
your deepest philosophy.

—Friedrich Nietzsche

Mind.

The mind is everything, what you think you become.

—Buddha

Happiness or misery is in the mind. It is the mind that lives.

—William Corbett

The trained mind is a rich mind.

—Robert Kiyosaki

The unfed mind devours itself.

—Gore Vidal

If you want to break through, your mind should be able to control your body. Your mind should be part of your fitness.

—Eliud Kipchoge

Fortune favors the prepared mind.

—Louis Pasteur

Values.

The aim of education is the knowledge, not of
facts, but of values.

—William S. Burroughs

A happy life is one which is in accordance with
its own nature.

—Seneca

I had chosen to use my work as a reflection of
my values.

—Sidney Poitier

Happiness is that state of consciousness which proceeds from the achievement of one's values.

—Ayn Rand

If you don't stick to your values when they're being tested, they're not values: they're hobbies.

—Jon Stewart

I am just a common man who is true to his
beliefs.

—John Wooden

The son put down the final card, smiled at the father, and said, "I understand what is next. I will see you tomorrow with my quotes on the body, mind, and values." The father nodded his assent, and the two men parted company.

The following morning was rainy, but the poor weather had no impact on the son's mood. He was excited to share the quotes he had collected. After father and son bought their coffee and were seated at the now very familiar table, the son pulled out his index cards and began to read:

Body.

If anything is sacred, the human body is sacred.

—Walt Whitman

Your body is your most priceless possession.
Take care of it.

—Jack LaLanne

Physical fitness is not only one of the most important keys to a healthy body, it is the basis of dynamic and creative intellectual activity.

—John F. Kennedy

The mind shapes the body, the body shapes the mind.

—Amy Cuddy

You need to listen to your body because your
body is listening to you.

—Phil McGraw

If we could give every individual the right amount of nourishment and exercise, not too little and not too much, we would have found the safest way to health.

—Hippocrates

Mind.

To the mind that is still, the whole universe surrenders.

—Lao Tzu

The mind is what the mind is fed.

—David J. Schwartz

A man is but the product of his thoughts. What he thinks, he becomes.

—Mahatma Gandhi

It is when the discomfort strikes that they realize a strong mind is the most powerful weapon of all.

—Chrissie Wellington

The more things that you read the more things
you will know, the more that you learn the more
places you will go!

—Dr. Seuss

Books open your mind, broaden your mind, and strengthen you as nothing else can.

—William Feather

Values.

When your values are clear to you, making decisions becomes easier.

—Roy E. Disney

Just as your car runs more smoothly and requires less energy to go faster and farther when the wheels are in perfect alignment, you perform better when your thoughts, feelings, emotions, goals, and values are in balance.

—Brian Tracy

Values are like fingerprints. Nobody's are the same, but you leave them all over everything you do.

—Elvis Presley

Strong beliefs win strong men, and then make them stronger.

—Richard Bach

Your core values are the deeply held beliefs that authentically describe your soul.

—John C. Maxwell

Open your arms to change but don't let go of
your values.

—Dalai Lama

"Well done," the father said. "Now tell me what you have learned."

The son paused for a moment to consider his response. "To be the best version of myself I must exercise my body, rest it, and fill it with good fuel. Trying to be my physical best does not mean comparing myself to other people or trying to reach an unrealistic physical standard; it means setting my own goals and trying to achieve them. My mind is also a muscle. I must exercise it by reading, learning, and getting out of my mental comfort zone. I need to fill my mind with positive fuel and healthy self-talk because my mind is an input-impacts-output system. I can't expect to generate positive outcomes by filling my mind with negative thoughts and images."

The son reflected for a moment while taking a sip of his coffee before continuing. "My values are my core beliefs that allow me to determine right from wrong. They help me make the right choice when I'm faced with a difficult decision and help me get back on track when I make mistakes. Living in harmony with my values is the only way to find lasting success and happiness."

The father smiled broadly at his response and nodded in agreement. "Your body is the vehicle, your mind is the engine, and your values are the guidance system," he said. "When you have a healthy body, a strong mind, and are living in harmony with your core values, you have reached the Golden Triangle; you have become the best version of yourself and created your best opportunity for success."

After the father finished, the son said nothing. He had adapted to the older man's habit of not filling silence with needless talk when the point had been made and the lesson was complete. Then it dawned on him that there would be no further lessons. This saddened him slightly because he had enjoyed these conversations much more than he thought he would. The Six Lessons did not seem condescending or judgmental. In fact, they did not feel like teaching at all. It was more like the father had guided his learning and asked him questions. Sensing the son's changing mood, the father asked, "Are you OK?"

"Everything is fine," the young man replied philosophically. "It's just that I'm going to miss our discussions now that they are done."

The father smiled; this admission was very nice to hear. They had come a long way since the difficult conversation they'd had at the start.

"I have enjoyed our talks as well, but I am afraid we aren't quite finished yet."

The son was puzzled. "I thought there were only six lessons?"

"Indeed," the father said, "but I would like for you to spend the final week thinking of all you have learned. After you have done that, we need to get together once more to share your perspectives."

The son smiled because, once again, he could see the father's now very familiar style of teaching. "I see," he replied. "I will think it all through before we meet back here one more time."

They shook hands and planned to meet the following week. As the father headed off to work, the son sat down, opened his notebook, and began to write:

Key Learning Points: The Sixth Lesson

- Becoming the best version of yourself gives you the best possible chance to succeed.
- In order to become the best version of yourself, you must focus on your body, mind, and values: the Golden Triangle.
- You must commit to healthy and realistic physical goals. Do not compare yourself to others but try to reach your personal best body at any age.
- Your mind is also a muscle. Feed it positive fuel and exercise it daily.
- The mind is an input-impacts-output system. Negativity and mental junk food make it weak. Positivity and healthy self-talk strengthen it.
- Thoughts and ideas are extremely powerful because whatever you focus on expands. If you focus on positivity, you will get positive outcomes; if you focus on negativity, that is what will happen.
- Ethical values help you make the right choice when you are faced with a difficult decision.
- Your values will also help you get back on track when you make mistakes.
- People who do not live in harmony with their core beliefs or create artificial, unethical values rarely sustain happiness or success.
- Your body is the vehicle, your mind is the engine, and your values are the guidance system.

Reader Quotes

Reader Key Learning Points

_____

_____

_____

_____

_____

_____

_____

_____

_____

_____

_____

_____

_____

_____

_____

_____

_____

Reader Exercise Number Six

Write out an exercise goal:

Write out a nutrition goal:

Write out a sleep goal:

Write out a reading or podcast-listening goal:

Write out a minimum of three things you like about yourself in the third person:

Example: I like Susan. She is a trustworthy and supportive friend.

1.
2.
3.

Write out a minimum of three of your core values:

1.
2.
3.

The Final Lesson

The mediocre teacher tells. The good teacher explains. The superior teacher demonstrates. The great teacher inspires.
—William Arthur Ward

The father looked down at his watch. The son would be arriving to meet him in the next five minutes. The nerves and apprehension he had eight weeks earlier were now a thing of the past. He could not take credit for this. The son had decided to change on his own, and through that change had decided to reconnect with him. Given this second chance, the older man decided that he would be a better listener and ask more questions. He would be patient, supportive, and not quick to judge. In the wake of these changes, a new relationship had emerged between the father and son. They were focused on what was happening in the present and not what had happened in the past. The teacher smiled to himself as he thought about how fortunate he was to have the son want to spend time with him and be a part of his life.

The son looked at the time on his phone. Ten minutes earlier the tone had gone off, reminding him that he had fifteen minutes before seeing the father. He actually didn't need the reminder. Seeing him was now one of the favorite parts of his week. The father had changed, and he now felt supported and listened to. He knew that his teacher wanted to help him grow and accomplish his dreams. *The key was that I had to want to do better*, he thought. *Once I asked for his help, he was right there for me.* The Six Lessons had helped them rebuild their relationship. Despite everything that happened between them, he was happy to have the father in his life and for a chance at a new beginning.

They met on the sidewalk in front of the coffee shop. They had both arrived at the same time and shared a warm embrace. The hug felt good. Each of them had changed and gained a better understanding of the other over the past several weeks. They entered the shop and ordered coffee. After they paid and sat down at their now very familiar corner table, the father said, "It has been eight weeks since you asked to meet and we began the Six Lessons. So tell me, what have you learned?"

The son furrowed his brow for a moment in deep thought. He seemed concerned and uneasy about the answer he was about to give. "I knew you would start with that question, so I have been thinking about my answer for the entire week leading up to our meeting," he said. He paused to take a sip of his coffee. "Please don't take this the wrong way, but after really thinking about it, I'm not sure I learned anything I didn't already know. There was some nuance and detailed information, but it felt to me that the Six Lessons are things that I've always known at some level."

The father smiled. Rather than being disappointed, this was the answer he had secretly hoped to hear. "And that is the final lesson, my son," the father said. "The secrets of successful living are not, in fact, secrets at all; they are fundamentals. Once you understand them, you can accomplish whatever you set your mind to. The rest is up to you."

A slow smile crept across the younger man's face. "That's why you told me on the first day that the level to which I am motivated is the single biggest factor in determining how successful I will become."

"Exactly," said the father. "The Six Lessons are not complex, but it is up to each individual to apply them. Just knowing them won't accomplish anything."

The two men sat in comfortable silence for a moment before the father added, "I have a gift for you." He reached into his briefcase and produced all the index cards containing the quotes from each of the Six Lessons. "I'm aware that you have carefully written out your key learning points after each lesson," he said, "but I thought that maybe you would like to add our 'research' to your notebook, so you could have your own personal manual containing the Six Lessons and everything we talked about."

"Thank you," said the son excitedly. "I think that this may turn out to be one of the greatest gifts I have ever received."

The father looked directly at him and said, "The gifts that we give to ourselves but then share with others often are, my son. I wish you success on your journey. I will always be here for you if you need me."

The son could see the love and commitment in the father's glistening eyes, and his eyes reflected the same. "As I will for you, Dad. As I will for you."

About the Author

Bob Willoughby was raised as the eldest son of two therapists in the foothills of the Blue Ridge Mountains in Charlottesville, Virginia.

After graduating with a degree in psychology from Randolph Macon College near Richmond, he landed at his favorite radio station as an entry-level account executive and felt like he had discovered the perfect job.

Following a successful twenty-one-year career in radio sales, he was promoted to general manager during the economic downturn of 2008. He quickly learned the importance of attitude, innovation, and creativity during this difficult time. He and his team embraced new sales structures and digital opportunities that greatly improved his market's profitability despite the recession.

Willoughby was recognized as one of Radio Ink's Best Managers in Radio for 2009. He served on the Virginia Association of Broadcaster's Executive Board from 2011 to 2014 and has lobbied Congress on behalf of the broadcast industry. In 2013 he served as VAB president. A participant in numerous executive leadership and coaching programs, Willoughby used that experience to create the VAB's "Best of the Best" Coaching Program for Broadcast Leadership in 2013, and he continues to contribute his time to it each year. In 2016 he received the CT Lucy Distinguished Service Award for Broadcast Leadership in the state of Virginia.

Many of his employees and coaching program participants have advanced into senior management and major market positions within the broadcast industry. He has been invited as a guest panelist to discuss career development, sales, leadership, and broadcasting at Virginia Commonwealth University and Howard University.

Residing in Midlothian, Virginia, with the girl of his dreams and their blended family of four kids, he is happily employed as the president of SummitMedia Richmond.

A former college basketball player and beer league ice hockey participant, he loves to ski, play golf, and watch sports every chance he gets.

Made in the USA
Middletown, DE
23 January 2021